Let's EXPLORE

baby einstein®

With Baby

A Parent's Activity Guide

The WALT DISNEP Company

Hyperion Books for Children, New York
Copyright © 2004 by The Baby Einstein Company, LLC.
All Rights Reserved.
Baby Einstein and the Boy's Head Logo are trademarks of The Baby Einstein Company, LLC. All Rights Reserved.
EINSTEIN and ALBERT EINSTEIN are trademarks of The Hebrew University of Jerusalem. All Rights Reserved.
For information address Hyperion Books for Children, 114 Fifth Avenue, New York, New York 10011-5690.
Printed in China
Library of Congress Cataloging Card Number on file.
ISBN 0-7868-3797-7

Visit www.hyperionbooksforchildren.com and www.babyeinstein.com

Great Minds Start Little.™

A Star Is Born

Reinforce words you use on a daily basis with a special picture book starring Baby. Take photos of Baby performing her everyday routine: capture her feeding herself in her high chair, playing with stacking rings, taking a bath, napping in her crib, and spending time with playmates or pets. Mount the photos in a sturdy scrapbook and add captions to create a story line that follows Baby through-out the day. For a book that is sure to become a favorite bed-time story, save a photo of Baby asleep in her crib for the last page of your book. Add a caption that's sure to elicit a happy ending to the evening: "Time for sweet Hannah to close her eyes and go to bed. Good night, Hannah."

Take pictures at your next play date of Baby and her friends enjoying different activities—bouncing balls, shaking rattles, blowing bubbles, stacking blocks, and playing instruments. Place the photos in a photo album that you've entitled "My Friends." Look through the album together, pointing to Baby's playmates, saying their names, and explaining what they're doing: "There's Amelia. She's playing with a blue ball." Add photos to the album every few months to capture your child's playing more advanced games and performing new actions that Baby couldn't undertake a few months earlier. In addition to making a terrific storybook that will help increase vocabulary, the photo album of Baby's friends will become a wonderful keepsake documenting your child's early years.

Create a memory game that features photos of your toddler, his friends, and his pets. Make two color copies for each photo you have. Cut color copies to fit onto fronts of old playing cards, then paste images onto the cards. To play the game, place all cards facedown on a table and ask your child to turn over two cards at a time. If he doesn't uncover two matching images, he must return the cards to a facedown position and keep uncovering two cards at a time until he makes a pair. This game sharpens memory skills and builds an understanding of pairs and matching like items.

⬤ Toddlers love to dress up in silly costumes and accessorize with bandannas, boas, scarves, wigs, hats, tiaras, wands, masks, and costume jewelry. Shop thrift stores and consignment shops for inexpensive, gently used Halloween costumes and fun dress-up clothes, then take photos of your child decked out in costumes that she's put together herself. Sit together and talk about each of the imaginary characters she's created, and encourage her to come up with a silly story for each photo or a thrilling tale that strings all of the characters together. Take careful notes, so that you can transcribe her story line into a scrapbook containing her character photos. She'll love reaching for a storybook that contains an exciting adventure straight from her imagination!

⬤ If you have a digital camera and computer with a color printer, you can create your own dictionary picture books of common vocabulary words. Although you don't need a digital camera to create these books, which simply feature photographs of common household items, a digital camera will prevent you from spending money on several rolls of film and save you the cost of getting the photos developed. Start by taking close-up photos of objects that suit a particular theme: fruits and vegetables; toys (rattles, blocks, dolls, teddy bears, and rubber duckies); articles of Baby's clothing (shirts, pants, bibs, dresses, and mittens); or household furniture (tables, chairs, couches, dressers, and beds). Download your digital images onto the computer, placing a few photos on each page of your document, and typing in the name of the items for each photo. Print out pages and mount them in a scrapbook that has sturdy, easy-to-turn pages. Create several picture books, each with a different theme, to reinforce the names of everyday objects for your child.

Animal Adventures

Teach animal names and sounds, using animal crackers and the "Old MacDonald's Farm" song. Sit Baby in her high chair and spread out several animal crackers. As you sing about each animal, pick up the corresponding cracker and make it dance atop her food tray. It won't be long before she can pick out the corresponding cracker as soon as she hears you sing the animal's name.

Create a storybook with your toddler, using pictures of your pets. If you don't have pets, ask elementary-age cousins to send photos of their furry friends to your little one. Children love to write about animals, so invite them to enclose a special letter detailing how they feed and care for their pets. Help your child compose a letter to his cousins, thanking them for their pet stories and asking follow-up questions about their animals. For cousins who live far away from you, this is a great way to start a pen-pal correspondence that could last for years.

You don't need to spend a lot of money or travel too far from home to go on an animal adventure that will delight your kids. Even a simple field trip to a nearby lake or forest can give them the opportunity to see and hear ducks, frogs, fish, squirrels, deer, and many interesting insects. Brush up on local animals with Baby Einstein's *Neighborhood Animals* book and see how many you can find on your field trip. To make it really feel like an adventure, bring along binoculars, a magnifying glass, a library book about regional wildlife, and a mini notebook for recording important animal findings and illustrations.

Fill up an inflatable kiddie pool with water and items to create your child's very own backyard pond. Add pond dwellers, like rubber duckies and plastic fish, turtles, dragonflies, and water bugs. Use green sponges to create floating lily pads for a few plastic frogs. Encourage your toddler to "quack," "ribbit," and "glub, glub" as he splashes about with his pond friends.

Enjoy a safari right in your own home, using stuffed animal and puppet monkeys, zebras, lions, tigers, and other exotic animals. Baby will love hearing you mimic the sounds of the animals as you put on a show for her, while your toddler will enjoy putting on a show for you. Expose your child to real-life images of these creatures in their natural habitats by incorporating the Baby Einstein *Animal Discovery Cards* into your game. To add another dimension to your safari adventure, check your local library's audio section for CDs or cassettes of jungle sounds.

Find out if there are any farms in your area that are open to the public. Aside from hearing the "oinks," "moos," and "neighs" of farm animals in person, your kids may even get the chance to see cows being milked, chickens laying eggs, pigs nursing a litter of piglets, and horses being groomed.

Nurturing With Nature

Baby will love exploring the many textures, colors, and scents your yard has to offer. Discover the uplifting scents and exciting textures of pine needles and pinecones. Tickle him with blades of grass and let him experience the thrill of crawling over a cool lawn and taking in its fresh scent. Point out squirrels, crows, and birds, and imitate their sounds. Take a few moments to absorb all that your property has to offer; rediscover it through your baby's eyes and consider the many science lessons it can provide about your region's animals, plants, and climate in the months to come.

Discover silly noises you can make with items found in nature. Bite into an apple or jump into a pile of leaves to let Baby hear what "crunch" sounds like. Make a blade of wet grass "squeak" or pebbles "plunk" into a brook. Listen to the wind "swoosh" and the rain go "pitter-patter." Take a walk in the backyard or in your neighborhood to find unique sounds that will make your baby giggle.

Here's a novel idea for a rainy-day adventure—go outside! Take your umbrellas and galoshes out during a light rain for a unique, multisensory experience. Encourage your child to feel the rain on his hands and face, and catch raindrops in his mouth. Listen to the gentle pitter-patter on your umbrella; spin your umbrellas around and hear the different effects the rain makes at varying speeds. If you don't mind the mess, splash around in puddles and talk about the sounds you make. Look for common rainy-day creatures, such as slugs, worms, and toads. Warm up by spending the rest of your rainy day at the library to find out more about these newfound friends.

Children are natural collectors and—naturally—love to collect items from nature! Take them on an outdoor adventure, whether it be to a popular hiking site, a simple wooded area in your town, or even your backyard. Bring a basket to collect unusual flowers, attractive leaves, and interesting nuts and seeds. Once home, use a plant or flower press to preserve the collection. Check out a few field guides from the local library—older children will especially love to play detective, tracking down clues about the "unidentified suspects" in their collection.

Once identified, they may want to glue their pressed naturals into a nature walk scrapbook or onto construction paper to create a one-of-a-kind wall hanging for their room.

★ Ask friends and family members across the country to send scenic postcards representative of their hometowns, with messages about what their neighborhood and climate is like and about the plants, animals, and insects that inhabit their neck of the woods. Place postcards in a photo album with sleeves that allow you to see the backs and fronts of the cards when you turn the pages of your neighborhoods-around-the-country storybook.

★ Visiting local garden centers and botanical gardens is a wonderful way to expose your child to the sights, smells, and textures of flowers, herbs, and shrubs. Make a game out of finding shapes on plants (such as heart-shaped lilacs, star-shaped columbines, and oval basil leaves) or ask them to  track down plants representing every color in the rainbow (such as red roses, orange lilies, yellow daffodils, green hostas, blue hydrangeas, purple irises, and pink snapdragons).

Shaping Up

★ Keep Baby occupied as he gets his diaper changed by hanging a mobile of plastic cookie cutters over his changing area. If his changing table is near a window, simply suspend a plastic hanger from the curtain rod, using plastic chain links. Add cookie cutters to the base of the hanger, using more links. When Baby starts getting fussy, simply distract him by pointing out the star, circle, heart, and triangle shapes dancing overhead.

Introduce Baby to everyday shapes, using common household items. Collect round balls, oval place mats, square books, triangular plastic hangers, empty rectangular tissue boxes, and heart-shaped lids from candy containers. Place these items in a plastic storage box, talking about the shape of each, and ask your child to pick out the shape as you call it out. Carry her with you and go from room to room, pointing out the many shapes that surround her.

It's easy for children to get antsy when sitting down to eat, so keep fussiness to a minimum by serving up a meal of shapes! Just before mealtime, ask your child to help you find an array of edible shapes in your kitchen, such as oval hard-boiled eggs, round tomato slices, triangular tortilla chips, crescent-shaped bananas, square cheese slices, and rectangular graham crackers. Your child will enjoy the sense of independence she gains from picking out her own menu (and will probably stay seated at the table until she's finished her meal!). When you run out of ideas for finding already existing food shapes, simply make your own shapely creations with cookie cutters: create circular sandwiches, heart-shaped ham slices, and star-shaped apple slices.

Make a shape sorter, using a shoe box and cookie cutters. Use a pencil to trace around plastic cookie cutters you've positioned on the box lid; cut out shapes with a utility knife, then replace the lid on the box. Your child will spend hours fitting the cookie cutters into the holes, removing the lid to shake out the cutters, and then replacing the lid to start the game all over again.

Exploring Math and Science

Playing with spinning toys builds coordination, aids in sensory motor development, and sets the stage for scientific exploration—so take one for a spin! Make your own spinning top with poster board, a plastic coffee-can lid, and a skewer stick. Trace around the lid on the poster board and cut out a circle. Paint a swirling spiral or other whimsical design onto the poster board circle. Alternatively, decorate with magazine cutouts of baby faces or even color-copied cutouts of your own baby's face. Use a nail to poke a hole through the poster board and lid. Slide a blunt-edged chopstick through both holes, and you're ready to start spinning. Watch your baby's reaction to the top spinning before him: his gaze will be fixed on the mesmerizing color in motion.

Puzzles are great tools for demonstrating how smaller parts fit together to create a whole. Color-copy a favorite photo of your child or pet, enlarging it to fit the size of a standard paper plate. Use a pencil to trace around the plate onto the color-copied image, centering the image as desired, then cut out the image and mount it on the paper plate. Cut the paper plate into four or five pieces. Mix up the pieces and show Baby how they fit together to make a complete picture.

Find whimsical plastic children's place mats at thrift shops and garage sales and cut them up into several large pieces. These make great toys to keep kids busy while waiting at the doctor's office and can be easily transported in a resealable plastic bag. Once your kids have mastered piecing together individual place-mat puzzles, put the pieces of two or three different puzzles into the same plastic bag; they'll enjoy the challenge of sorting and matching up the mixed-up pieces.

Teach Baby about opposites by demonstrating how things work around the house: the light switch goes on and off, doors let you go in and out of the house, dresser drawers open and close, running water can be warm or cold, drinking glasses can be empty or full, and sweatshirt zippers pull up and down, while suitcase zippers move left to right.

Fill an empty paper milk carton with water and drop in favorite plastic toys. Freeze, then peel off the paper carton to reveal a frozen block of toys. Let your child see and touch the cold block and discuss how it feels and what she sees. Place the block in a sink to watch the ice melt in hot water and magically release her toys. This scientific exercise will introduce her to the liquid, frozen, and gas states of water.

Future architects will love constructing forts and playhouses from large cardboard boxes—a good exercise in spatial relationships. Call around and see if local appliance stores, electronic outlets, or home-supply stores have any large boxes you could take off their hands. Use a utility knife to fashion a front door that's just your toddler's size and add a few windows. Sit down with your toddler to discuss your construction plans. Where does he want to put the house? Is it for indoor or outdoor play? What would he like his cardboard house to look like on the outside? What would he like to put inside the house? How many boxes will you need to tape together to create the house he's envisioning? Your toddler will love offering his input and insights and will gain confidence in his decision-making skills. You may want to suggest different ways to cover or decorate the box's exterior (using construction paper, wrapping paper, favorite stickers, or trading cards), as well as fun ideas for decorating inside (towels for curtains, beanbag chairs, transistor radio, small table, a battery-operated camping lamp, and glow-in-the dark stars on the walls).

 Stir up some magic right in your kitchen with an easy-to-make bubble-blowing solution. Mix together 1/2 cup water with a tablespoon of dishwashing liquid (do not use laundry detergent or detergent designed for a dishwasher, as they are toxic). For bubble wands, experiment with funnels, slotted spoons, and potato mashers for different results.

Color Their Worlds

Many game spinners from children's board games feature bright colors or numbers on their faces. Although Baby is too young to enjoy a board game, a game spinner to help her learn the names of colors and numbers may be just her speed! To play with these "spinning flash cards," simply spin the arrow and call out the number or color the arrow lands on.

Encourage your child to come up with his own rhymes and songs about colors and sounds. Use "rattle jars" to reinforce the names of colors. Find as many jars as needed to represent each color found in a package of construction paper. Selecting a different color for each jar, roll up a piece of construction paper (cut to fit height of jar) and place it inside so that it covers the sides of the glass. Place different noisemakers, like rattles, large jingle bells, or keys, in each jar. Then play musical color games with your rainbow of rattle jars: "Pick up the big blue jar and shake it, shake it, near and far."

Find a bunch of solid-colored chiffon scarves or lightweight pieces of fabric that will float when thrown up in the air. As you throw them in the air to float down to Baby, name the scarf's color: "Whee! There's a BLUE scarf that's flying way up high. It's floating down to Michael. You can catch it if you try!" Play peekaboo with each scarf, reinforcing the names of colors: "Where's Julia? Is she hiding under the RED scarf? Peekaboo!"

Here's a great game to play when stuck inside on a rainy day. Select a crayon and scribble a patch of color on the page of a miniature notebook. Send your child on a colorful fact-finding mission, asking him to find as many items as he can in the house that match the color scribbled on his notebook page.

Serve food with a color theme to add some excitement to mealtime and learn about colors, bite by bite. Try a yellow breakfast, featuring scrambled eggs, apple juice, bananas, and melted cheese on a potato-bread slice. Enjoy a red lunch of spaghetti with tomato sauce, beets, cranberry juice, and sliced strawberries and raspberries. For dinner, you can even make the color brown exciting: meat loaf, baked potato, gravy, sautéed mushrooms, Bosc pears, chocolate milk, and gingerbread cookies for dessert.

Music to Their Ears

You can make homemade rattles, using yogurt containers, plastic water or juice bottles, and small, plastic kitchen containers. Fill containers with household items that are sure to clank and rattle: rice, shells, dried beans, popcorn kernels, candy sprinkles, or large wooden spools. Ensure that container lids are securely fastened for Baby's safety, then shake rattle to this song:

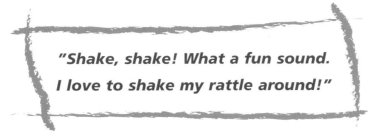

"Shake, shake! What a fun sound.
I love to shake my rattle around!"

Encourage Baby to shake the rattle herself.

Create a rattle that's also fun to cuddle. Remove the stuffing from a small stuffed animal. Replace stuffing with keys, then sew the toy shut. For crinkly rattles, fill stuffed toys with cellophane paper.

Baby will love discovering the different effects he can create by experimenting with a range of homemade drumsticks. Help him create his own beat with plastic spatulas, measuring spoons, plastic pail shovels, or toy xylophone mallets. For the baby who hasn't yet graduated to solid foods, here's a great way to ease his transition into the high chair: sit him in the high chair every day with his drumsticks and let him bang out a tune on the food tray.

Try to stump your kids with the "Guess the Sound" game. Cover a jar with construction paper and ask them to close their eyes as you put a mystery item inside. Shake the jar and have them guess just what it is you're shaking inside your jar. If they're stumped, give them subtle clues to help solve the mystery: "This is something you use to eat cereal. It has a long handle." Consider shaking a set of keys, metal measuring spoons, dried rice, large wooden spools, and other household items you can find "rattling around" in your pantry or junk drawers. Be sure to utilize items that won't pose choking hazards.

Toddlers will love keeping time to music with their very own set of maracas made from a potato-chip canister. Fill the canister halfway with rice or dried beans; replace the plastic lid and secure it with a strip of masking tape. Cover the canister with construction paper and let your child decorate the exterior with markers and crayons.

⭐ Turn empty, cylinder-shaped oatmeal boxes or empty coffee cans into a set of bongo drums. Hot-glue a long wooden spool between two of the boxes to create your bongo set. Decorate the drums with markers and crayons.

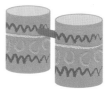

🥁 Mouth instruments will help your child learn how to maneuver her lips and tongue when taking measured breaths to blow out air. This is good practice for speech development. Cover one end of a cardboard toilet-paper roll with waxed paper; secure the paper with hot glue. Take turns making a "doo-doo-doo" kazoo sound into the open end. Try out favorite words, animal sounds, and silly songs with the kazoo. Your child will love to feel the words tickle her mouth as the sound reverberates in the tube. She will also enjoy tooting her horn through a plastic kitchen funnel or even into a disposable plastic cup. The amplified sounds she creates will provide endless amusement.

⭐ Discover the do-it-yourself drum corps that's hidden in your kitchen cabinets. March out those pots, pans, pie tins, empty cereal boxes, metal measuring cups, plastic mixing bowls, cookie sheets, and plastic pitchers for some percussive playtime. Empty formula canisters make great percussion instruments, providing a sturdy plastic drumming surface as well as a metal bottom for a steel drum sound. Sing this song as you drum together:

> *"Bum-dee-dee-bum, Billy's in a band.*
> *He can play the drums with his hands.*
> *Bum-dee-dee-bum, Billy's having fun—*
> *Drumming with those fingers and thumbs!"*

Seasonal Fun

Create paper snowflakes, using colorful metallic papers and glitter pens. Attach sparkly snowflakes to car windows out of Baby's reach to occupy him while he's in his car seat. Or dangle them from a plastic hanger to create a lovely winter mobile for him to gaze at in his room. Ensure that the mobile is positioned far out of Baby's reach. Consider updating the mobile each season: flowers for spring, smiling suns for summer, and colorful leaves for autumn.

Children are captivated by the touch, taste, and sight of snow, and all the magic that winter has to offer. If you don't live in a climate with cold winters, create your own "snow" in the bathtub with crushed ice—it's a great way for Baby to learn about the word "cold" and an opportunity for him to explore a new, slushy texture.

Add several drops of food coloring to a spray bottle of water and paint the snow outside with fun stars, smiley faces, numbers, letters, triangles, and other fun designs.

In autumn, go on a leaf hunt with your toddler. Collect an array of brilliant red, orange, and yellow leaves in different shapes and sizes. Arrange your child's collection between two sheets of waxed paper. Place a dish towel on top of the waxed paper and, using a warm setting, iron the towel on a warm setting to preserve the leaves. After you identify the leaves and learn a bit about the trees they came from, display the preserved leaves on your windows as fun, seasonal decorations or in picture frames to give as gifts or to decorate your child's bedroom.

Instead of buying one large Halloween pumpkin for your child to decorate, purchase several minigourds and give each one a different expression. Talk about the different faces she wants to create, such as happy, spooky, silly, sad, and scared ones. Sketch out her ideas on paper, giving thoughtful consideration to the shape of the gourd (round, hourglass, square, or oval) and how it will add to the effect she wants to create. Since carving is a lot of messy work and doesn't allow kids hands-on involvement, use markers, glitter pens, hats, and Halloween costume accessories to dress up your gourds instead.

It's easy to make your own snow globes, using large-sized baby food jars with tight-fitting lids. Use epoxy glue (or another waterproof glue) to adhere a plastic figurine to the inside of the jar lid. Let glue dry completely. Fill jar almost to top with distilled water, adding a drop or two of glycerine or baby oil. Add a pinch or two of white or silver glitter to create "snow," then permanently fasten the lid to the jar, turn it upside down, and enjoy the snowy scene. Homemade snow globes make wonderful stocking stuffers.

Enjoy a snowy treat on a summer day: Make snow cones with crushed ice and your child's favorite juice, for a treat that is not only tasty to toddlers but is also comforting to teething babies.

Create a holiday storybook starring your family. Older children can help you write text to accompany photos of your kids playing in the snow, sitting on Santa's lap, eating holiday cookies, wrapping presents, and decorating the Christmas tree. Sure to become a treasured family keepsake, this special storybook will be something your kids will look forward to reading every holiday season, no matter how old they are.